Dealing With

MY

STEPFAMILY

by Jane Lacey
Illustrated by Venitia Dean

W
FRANKLIN WATTS
LONDON•SYDNEY

Franklin Watts
First published in Great Britain in 2017 by The Watts Publishing Group

Credits
Series Editor: Sarah Peutrill
Series Design: Collaborate

ISBN 978 1 4451 5795 5

Printed in China

Franklin Watts
An imprint of
Hachette Children's Group
Part of The Watts Publishing Group
Carmelite House
50 Victoria Embankment
London EC4Y 0DZ

An Hachette UK Company
www.hachette.co.uk

www.franklinwatts.co.uk

MIX
Paper from
responsible sources
FSC® C104740

FSC
www.fsc.org

Contents

WHAT IS A STEPFAMILY?

If your mum or dad is living with a new partner or has married again, they make a new family called a stepfamily.

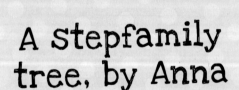

A stepfamily tree, by Anna

A stepfamily can be small – just you and your mum or dad plus your stepmum or dad. It can be big with lots of stepsisters and brothers.

You might have two mums – your own mum and your stepmum. You might have two dads, like Anna – your own dad and your stepdad.

4

Caden's mum, Helen

My stepdad, Don

Mum

Dad

My stepbrother, Caden

My half-sister, Carrie

My sister, Lily

Me

Anna's story

I am part of a stepfamily. When Mum and Dad got divorced, my sister Lily and I stayed with our mum. Then Mum got married again. Her new husband, Don, is our stepdad. Don's son Caden came to live with us. He's our stepbrother. So our mum is Caden's stepmum! Carrie is Mum and Don's little girl. We all think she is really sweet!

EVERYTHING'S CHANGING!

Jacob and his dad have been on their own for a long time. Now his dad's partner Gilly and her two children are moving in. Jacob doesn't want things to change.

Jacob's story

Dad and I are happy together. I like the way we do things. I don't mind seeing Gilly and her children sometimes, but I don't want them living here all the time. I don't see why things have to change.

6

what can Jacob do?

He can:

* talk to his dad and say he is worried about Gilly and the children being there all the time
* ask if he and his dad will still have time together.

what Jacob did

I told Dad I like it when it's just him and me at home. I don't want things to change. Dad said he loves me but he loves Gilly too. He wants to be with her as well as with me.

He promises we will still have time together - just him and me. I suppose I'll get used to sharing Dad.

MY STEPDAD'S NOT MY REAL DAD

Daniel's mum has married again and Daniel is having trouble accepting his new stepdad. He loves his own dad. He doesn't want another dad.

Will

Will is Daniel's friend

My mum and dad like having my friend Daniel round. He's always nice and polite to them. He even clears away his plate after supper! But he's different at his home. He's really rude to his stepdad.

Daniel's story

Geoff is only my stepdad. He's not my real dad but Geoff wants me to call him 'Dad'. Well, I won't! The only person I'll ever call 'Dad' is my real dad.

Geoff thinks he can boss me around and tell me what to do! I hope, if I'm disobedient and rude to him, he'll get fed up and go away. I'm afraid if I'm nice to him, he might stay. So I'm not nice to him and I don't call him anything.

Geoff

Daniel

what can Daniel do?

He can:
* ★ remember his stepdad loves his mum. It would make her unhappy if Geoff went away
* ★ ask if he can call Geoff by his name instead of 'Dad'
* ★ start to be polite to Geoff and treat him with respect.

What Daniel did

I know being rude to Geoff makes Mum unhappy so I have started to be more polite to him. I've even started doing what I'm told! Geoff and I get on much better. He doesn't mind me calling him 'Geoff' instead of 'Dad'. Mum is much happier now.

A stepdad's story

I love Ben and Sam's mum. I really like Ben and Sam, too. I want us all to be a happy family.

It has been difficult because they love their dad. They were afraid I wanted to take their dad's place. They didn't want to like me.

Now they know I don't want them to stop loving their dad. I just want them to like me, too. We are getting used to our new stepfamily. It's getting better all the time.

WILL MY STEPMUM STAY WITH US?

Riley's dad has a new partner, Jane. He says Jane is going to be Riley's new stepmother. But Riley is worried that Jane won't stay with them for long.

Emma

Riley

Riley's Story

My dad's ex-partner Emma lived with us for a long time. She was my stepmum and I really liked her. I was sad when she and Dad split up. Now I'm worried my new stepmum will leave us, too. I'm starting to like her a lot already.

12

What can Riley do?

She can:

★ tell her dad she is afraid her new stepmum will leave
★ ask how she can be sure Jane will stay and explain she felt sad when Emma left
★ say she doesn't want to feel sad like that again.

What Riley did

I told Dad how sad I was when Emma left. I cried and cried. I said, "How do I know Jane won't leave, too?"

But Dad said, "Jane and I are getting married." I'm going to be a bridesmaid! Now I know they both really want to stay together for a long time.

I FEEL LEFT OUT

Elliot is an only child. Now he has a new stepbrother and sister who play together all the time. This makes him feel left out.

Tom

Tom is Elliot's friend

I'm an only child, the same as my friend Elliot. It can be lonely at home sometimes. I wish I had a new stepbrother and sister like Elliot. But he said he feels lonelier than before!

Elliot

Elliot's story

My stepbrother and sister are used to playing together. They have lots of fun but they don't ask me to join in their games. They whisper and have secrets with each other.

I think my mum spoils them. She doesn't make them eat their vegetables and she even tidies their bedroom for them! I have to eat all my vegetables and tidy my own room. I think Mum loves them more than she loves me. I feel left out.

What can Elliot do?

He can talk to his mum:

* ★ tell her that he feels that she loves his stepbrother and sister more than him
* ★ tell her she seems to have fewer rules for them than for him
* ★ explain he feels lonely and left out.

What Elliot did

I told Mum how I felt. She said she would try to be fairer. Mum plays cards and games with us all and we have fun together. Sometimes I play with my stepbrother and sister without Mum now. Most days, Mum makes sure we spend time together - just Mum and me. I don't feel left out any more.

Amy also felt left out when she got new stepsisters.

A mum's story

When I got married again, my daughter Amy had a new stepdad and two stepsisters. I thought it would nice for her to have someone to play with. But Amy's stepsisters played together and Amy said she felt left out. Her stepsisters said Amy wouldn't join in their games. So I've started taking them all swimming and they have a great time. Now they know how much fun they can have together, they are playing together at home, too. Amy and I still have fun together when my stepdaughters visit their mum.

WHY DO I HAVE TO SHARE?

Tilly is used to having a bedroom of her own. Now she has to share her bedroom with her stepsister. But she doesn't want to share it.

Kerry

Eve

Tilly

Eve is Tilly's friend

When I go to play with my friend Tilly we always play in her bedroom. But now her stepsister Kerry is often there, too. Tilly's room is so full of Kerry's bed and all Kerry's stuff, there's hardly any room for us!

Tilly's story

I used to have my room all to myself. Now I have to share it with my stepsister, Kerry. She's older than me. She likes different things. There isn't really enough room for both of us.

When Eve comes round, Kerry's always there so now Eve and I play downstairs. But when Kerry has her friends round I still have to go downstairs! It's not fair!

Kerry wants a room of her own and so do I but there isn't another bedroom in our house.

What can Tilly do?

She can:

★ decide with her stepsister the times they can
  have the room to themselves
★ make their own private spaces in the room
★ remember it's hard for her stepsister to have to
  share, too.

What Tilly did

Kerry and I agreed that whoever has a friend
round gets the bedroom. Apart from that, I have the
bedroom to myself when I get in from school. It's
Kerry's after tea. We aren't very tidy but we keep
our things on our own sides of the room. Sometimes
we like being there together now.

Liam's Story

When Mum and I moved into Mum's partner's house, I had to share a room with his son, Benny. Benny's younger than me so we go to bed at different times. If I read with the light on, it wakes Benny up! Then he gets up early and wakes me up! So we fixed up a curtain between our beds. If Benny calls through the curtain, I don't mind. Sometimes I tell him stories if he can't get to sleep.

MY STEPMUM'S RULES AREN'T FAIR!

Leo doesn't like his stepmum's new rules. He thinks her rules are too strict and that they aren't fair. He argues with her all the time.

Harry

Harry is Leo's friend

My friend Leo thinks his stepmum is too strict. I don't think she is really. She only makes the same rules as my mum, like helping with the washing-up. Leo sticks to my mum's rules without a fuss when he's round at my house.

Leo

Leo's story

My stepmum treats me like a little kid. My stepbrothers are older than me and she sends me to bed earlier than them. She doesn't let me watch the programmes I want but she lets them watch what they like! When I go to stay with my mum, she lets me stay up late and we watch telly together. We eat chocolate, too, but my stepmum never lets me have chocolate! I argue with my stepmum and I say, "It's not fair! My mum lets me! You can ask my dad."

What can Leo do?

He can talk to his dad and stepmum together:

★ say why he thinks the rules aren't fair
★ talk about what his mum lets him do
★ see if they can all agree on some rules
★ when he has agreed to the rules, try to stick to them without arguing!

What Leo did

I talked to Dad and my stepmum about things like my bedtime, the washing-up and watching telly. Now Dad and I have agreed rules with my stepmum, I stick to them - most of the time! When I'm with my mum, she spoils me a bit. That's probably because she doesn't have to put up with me all the time!

Henry also felt he was treated differently to his stepsister.

Henry's story

My mum always wanted a little girl, but she just had me! When my stepdad's little girl Hester comes to stay, Mum makes a big fuss of her. She buys her clothes and presents every time she comes! I told Mum I feel as though she loves Hester more than me. Mum gave me a big hug. She said sorry and told me how much she loves me. I don't really mind if she spoils Hester - as long as she spoils me as well sometimes!

I LIKE MY STEPDAD BETTER THAN MY REAL DAD

Kyle gets on well with his stepdad. He is worried that his own dad would be unhappy if he knew.

Kyle and his stepdad

Kyle's story

I don't look forward to seeing my dad. We don't do anything much. He wants to know what is going on at home but he gets upset when I tell him! I really like my stepdad. He's good fun and he makes Mum happy. I feel bad for my dad but sometimes I think I like my stepdad better.

What can Kyle do?

He can:

* remember it is all right to love his stepdad
* tell his dad he doesn't want to talk about home with him
* ask his dad if they can do things together when he sees him.

What Kyle did

I told Dad I didn't want to talk about home. He said that was okay. I said I wanted to learn Judo on Saturdays. Dad found Judo classes near him. Now we are both learning Judo! It's brilliant. We both really enjoy it.

Kyle and his dad

WE'RE GOOD FRIENDS NOW

Arran and Bonny are stepbrother and sister. They didn't get on with each other at first.

Arran and Bonny's Story

Arran:
When I heard I was going to have a stepsister, I was disappointed. I wanted a stepbrother.

Bonny:
Yeah! And I wanted a stepsister. But I got Arran!

Arran:
I thought Bonny would only like girls' stuff - dolls and make-up and pink things.

Bonny:
I thought Arran would be crazy about football and have smelly socks.

Arran:
Actually, I really like riding my bike more than football. Bonny's got a cool bike, too, so we ride our bikes together.

Bonny: I love reading. Arran has lots of books and he lends me some. They are great. I lend him my books, too. It's like having a whole library at home!

Arran: Mostly, when Bonny has her friends round, I keep out of their way. And when I have my friends round, she keeps out of our way.

Bonny: But we had a joint swimming party for our birthdays. Our friends had a really good time together. So we know our friends get on well if they have to.

Arran: Bonny went on holiday with her mum for two weeks and I really missed her.

Bonny: I thought it would be great to have Arran out of the way when he visited his Gran, but I missed him, too.

Arran: Bonny and I didn't think we would like each other. But now we are good friends.

GLOSSARY

Divorce
A husband and wife are divorced when they sign papers that mean they are not married any more.

Fair
A rule or a decision is fair when it is good for everyone involved.

Lonely
People sometimes feel lonely when they have to spend a lot of time on their own.

Married
Two people are married when they sign papers that make them husband and wife.

Partners
Two people who live together but are not married are called partners.

Private
You are private when you choose to be alone or keep something to yourself.

Respect
You respect someone when you understand them and are kind to them.

Rules
Rules are things that you must obey. For example:
★ bedtime at 8 p.m.
★ finish homework before watching television.

Share
You share when you tell or give things to other people and you don't keep things to yourself.

Stepfamily
A stepfamily is made when two people who already have children get together to make a new family.

Further information

For children

www.childline.org.uk
Tel: 0800 1111
Childline is a free helpline for children in the UK. You can talk to someone about any problem and they will help you to sort it out.

www.kidshealth.org
Confused, sad, mad, glad? Check out the 'Feelings' section to learn about these emotions and others – and how to deal with them.

For readers in Australia and New Zealand

www.cyh.com
Loads of online information about all sorts of issues.

www.kidshelp.com.au
Tel: 1800 55 1800
Kidshelp is the free helpline for children in Australia. You can talk to someone about any problem.

www.kidsline.org.nz
A helpline run by specially trained young volunteers to help kids and teens deal with troubling issues and problems.

For parents

www.parentlineplus.org.uk
Helpline for parents:
0808 800 2222
ParentLine Plus offers advice, guidance and support for parents who are concerned about their children.

Note to parents and teachers: Every effort has been made by the Publishers to ensure these websites are suitable for children, that they are of the highest educational value and that they contain no inappropriate or offensive material. However, because of the nature of the Internet, it is impossible to guarantee that the contents of these sites will not be altered. We strongly advise that Internet access is supervised by a responsible adult.

INDEX

Notes for parents, carers and teachers

Some children will enjoy being part of a stepfamily. Others will find it difficult. There are many ways parents, carers and teachers can help children to deal with their stepfamily.

- Having a good relationship with their natural parents can help children to get on with their step-parents.
- It helps children to know that their dad will always be Dad and their mum will always be Mum whatever happens.
- It helps to have special times alone with your natural child.
- Parents can help by not quizzing their child about what goes on in their stepfamily, although don't avoid talking about it either.

Page 6 Jacob's story
Jacob doesn't want his dad's partner and her children to move in with them. He wants his dad to himself.

- Talking about feelings and discussing ways to cope can help children to deal with change.

Page 9 Daniel's story
Daniel doesn't want his stepdad to replace his new dad so he is being rude and disobedient.

- Expecting children to behave politely and with respect however they feel and then treating them the same way is a helpful step towards getting on better together.

Page 12 Riley's story
Riley is worried that her new stepmum will leave her and her dad.

- Children are often affected by a new relationship and need love and consideration when decisions are being made.

Page 15 Elliot's story
Elliot thinks his mum favours his stepbrother and sister and he feels left out.

- It helps to be fair to every child in a stepfamily and treat them all the same.

Page 19 Tilly's story
Tilly is finding it difficult sharing her bedroom with her older stepsister.

- Agreeing rules and organising personal space can help when children have to share a bedroom.

Page 23 Leo's story
Leo resents his stepmum's rules and thinks she is stricter than his own mum.

- Children can play one parent off against the other to get their own way. Rules that are fair and reasonable should be stuck to by parents and children.

Page 26 Kyle's story
Kyle is worried because he has more fun with his stepdad than his own dad.

- Planning a shared activity or learning something new together can help build a good relationship with your child if you don't live with them.

Page 28 Playscript: Arran and Bonny's story
Children could 'perform' the parts in this simple playscript. They could also write and perform their own play about living in a stepfamily.

These are the list of contents for the titles in the Dealing With series.

Dealing With Bullying

I feel left out * What is bullying? * I'm bullied about the way I speak * Big girls at school hurt me! * My friends are bullies * They make fun of my lunch! * I'm always in trouble! * My friend bullies his brother * How to get help if you are being bullied * We beat bullying: playscript.

Dealing With Our New Baby

I don't want a new baby! * Expecting a baby * I'm worried that Mum and the baby won't be all right * Getting ready for the baby * The new baby's boring! * I'm jealous of the new baby * My baby brother's a nuisance! * I want to help! * Watching a baby grow * My little sister always gets her own way! * Will my stepdad still love me? * Our new baby: playscript

Dealing With My Parents' Divorce

My home isn't a happy place to be any more * What is divorce? * My parents are getting a divorce * I feel angry with my mum and dad * Is my parents' divorce my fault? * What's going to happen to me? * I'm ashamed about my parents' divorce * How can I love both my mum and dad? * Will we be happy again? * It happened to us: playscript.

Dealing With My Stepfamily

What is a stepfamily? * Everything's changing! * My stepdad's not my real dad * Will my stepmum stay with us? * I feel left out * Why do I have to share? * My stepmum's rules aren't fair! * I like my stepdad better than my real dad * We're good friends now: playscript

Dealing With When People Die

I don't know what is happening! * What is death? * I don't want to say goodbye! * What happens at a funeral? * I'm angry with my brother for leaving me * Will I ever stop feeling sad? * I'm afraid I will die too * My parents don't love me now * I miss granddad too * How can I remember someone special? * When our friend died: playscript

Dealing With Racism

I'm new in this country and at school * We are different and the same * I'm left out * What is racism? * It's my name too! * Celebrations * Racism is making my friend unhappy * I'm in a gang * I'm scared * Racism in schools * We dealt with racism: playscript